Zen And Mindfulness With Dogs

AF189152

To Mali

Holger Junghardt

Zen And Mindfulness With Dogs

Bibliographical Information of the Deutsche Nationalbibliothek
This publication is listed in the Deutsche Nationalbibliographie of the
Deutsche Nationalbibliothek; detailed bibliographical information
can be accessed under http: //dnb.d-nb.de

© 2018 Holger Junghardt
Printing, Production and Layout: BoD – Books on Demand
ISBN: 978-3-7448-6652-1

content

Introduction

Another dog book? Sure! Whether you want to bring a dog into your home or you already own one, this little booklet can help you to understand dogs better. Especially if you have no idea at all, you will get a first overview at a small price.

The title may suggest religion or even esotericism, but that is not the case. Rather, the findings from Zen and from Buddhism are used to get a different view of the story.

I myself went through an apprenticeship as a dog trainer in the dog school of Rita Kampmann, Munich, Germany, and subsequently trained myself as a Dog Psychologist nTR with Thomas Riepe. I have gained my practical experience with dogs with my Beagle Mali, who got 18 years old, as well as in the dog school, in a dog daycare and with numerous dog guests at my home.

My Buddhist background began in the last century. Since then, I have been practicing mindfulness in everyday life, meditation, and have attended retreats and Dharma lectures.

Of course, reading this little booklet is not enough to solve all problems with dogs. There are very good dog books, but they are hard to find in the mass of publications. In the appendix you will find an overview of recommended literature. Each of these books is fully recommendable.

We all have a personal relation to dogs, so I will call them "he", for all female and male dogs.

If even one dog should gain a happier life through this writing, the trouble of writing has already paid off.

Do I have to become a Zen monk?

It would not be the worst, but no, you don't. The essential realization that is experienced after more or less long Zen practice is that there is no independent existence. Consequently, there is no ego and thus there is no separation between subject and object. This is not intellectually perceptible, but some examples may show what it is about.

There is a wave in the great wide sea, and this wave thinks she is the most beautiful, the best, and the greatest wave that ever existed. And she becomes arrogant because she considers the other waves to be inferior and is now suddenly afraid of not existing anymore. If she did not think this way, she would just see that she was only part of the great sea and did not exist independently, but was connected to all the other waves. She consists even of non-wave parts, namely, only of the substance of the ocean.

Buddhism formulates this in the Heart-Sutra in the famous statement: "Form is emptiness, and emptiness is form".

The realization from this example is that there is no independent existence, even if one thinks there is. In addition, this thinking creates many problems because one does not recognize reality and develops negative qualities such as hatred and greed.

Probably this small intellectual bridge has not yet led to the great realization that the world is like that. Not for nothing, you have to sit in Zen for a very long period of time and just watch. The mind will hopefully be confused by a koan so far as to abandon its intellectual objections.

But if there really is no separation between the subject and the object, then I do all the bad things I do unto others to myself. And that is why it is necessary to lead a mindful life.

What is the meaning of mindfulness?

It is easy to see that all the bad things that you do unto others come back to you again. For example, you have a dispute with someone and you are increasingly raging. You decide to leave the place of the quarrel after violent controversy - still in rage - and in blindness of rage you run into the lane of a vehicle that has a little more energy than you and that is therefore very painful. Or think of old slapstick films, where two opponents continue to pursue their revenge and things get more and more evil, until they finally destroy all their belongings, and come at the happy ending to the conclusion that something has fundamentally gone wrong.

In ethics, therefore, there is also the golden rule: do unto others as you would have them do unto you. This is perfectly logic when one considers that there is no separation between subject and object. Compassion with other beings is therefore nothing other than compassion with oneself.

Mindfulness means to practice compassion. Compassion implies the realization that all living creatures want to be happy. Compassion forbids hatred and greed. But other thoughts can be detrimental to compassion. Many people believe their view of things is the right thing. Out of this belief, because they want only the right and the best, many things happen that cause great suffering. This begins with parents who want only the best, and ends up in the collective beliefs of states to do just the right thing and instigate gruesome wars.

So that this blindness does not arise, one should observe much more mindfully, instead of constructing its own world. Whoever thinks does not live in reality. Because you can only think about the past and the future. The present moment can only be experienced or displaced by thoughts. "I think, therefore I am," was once proclaimed by Mr. Descartes (he put it as an intellectual in Latin: "cogito, ergo sum"). Non cogito, ergo sum, I say. Because only in non-thinking can reality be experienced. Of course you should not give up thinking. But instead of missing the reality in the rushing of thoughts, the mind should only be used as a tool. And with a tool should not be played.

The hammer has been designed for hammering nails. Whoever is constantly playing around with it, does not have to complain later, if the valuable porcelain breaks, when the hammer glides carelessly out of ones hand.

And how does it work in practice?

You can sit down for hours as you would in the Zen monastery, watching your thoughts and ultimately experiencing non-thinking. To achieve this, you can only observe your breath and let your mind wander.

In order to finally confuse the intellect and let it rest, one can use a question which can't be answered by the mind. At some point, the mind will give up and this is the moment of non-thinking. These questions are called Koans. If you read this little book until the end, you will encounter such a koan.

It is more important to be mindful in everyday life. In addition to the practice of compassion, every action should be carried out at present. When I breathe, I breathe, when I eat, I eat and when I run, I run.

A master of this discipline are, by the way, dogs, but also all other animals. They make no reproaches about the past and do not worry about the future. They are content with their lives, are fond of eating and walking around, and their only possession is perhaps a toy.

The observation of dogs is a perfect training for mindful behavior.

Just be aware of all the prejudices about dogs. Mindful observation means to perceive reality unfiltered. Careful handling means accepting the nature of the dog.

Since this is very difficult, and, in some cases it is advisable to use the understanding in dealing with dogs, the most important questions about dogs are to be answered on the following pages.

What is the nature of dogs?

First, it is helpful to know that dogs are descended from the wolf and are still similar to them. For many thousand years man has changed the nature of the wolf to its own benefit, thus creating the different races. They have bred dogs, for example, which are especially suited for hunting, or which are fine for guarding or suitable for the herding of sheep herds. For this purpose, they have selected specific characteristics of wolves and strengthened them by breeding.

Wolves live in family associations. They raise their puppies, who later leave the group to form their own association. An excluded wolf moves on alone and founds a new family. In the family, there is division of labor and everyone contributes to the search for food and security. Hunting is best done in a group. The food is quickly devoured, everyone tries to get something off. Even the puppies get to the collected food and do not allow the family head to take the lead (quite the contrary - the wolf will always feed their puppies first at a time of scarcity).

In addition to chasing game, wolves regularly roam their territory, mark the borders (often with imposing gestures) and fend off competitors. When another wolf enters a foreign territory, he is first driven out by threatening gestures. Only when the stranger does not react, he is attacked. Mostly, he will try to appease the attacker and run away.

Possibly they were excluded wolves, which first approached human settlements and fed themselves from waste. Some of them were captured by humans and used for hunting, guarding, herding etc. These domesticated animals were used for breeding, and this way our domestic dog was born.

Wolves and dogs perceive the world through their nose. They can smell at least 6,000 times better than we do. The primary perception of the world is fundamentally different from that of humans. The sense of hearing is also finer and more developed than that of humans. Dogs can see very well, especially in the twilight, but the color vision is limited, and movements are perceived better than static impressions. The sense of touch is especially supported by the tactile hair around the snout.

Otherwise, wolves sleep long and extensively and so do our house dogs (up to 20 hours a day). After getting up, they shake themselves.

The typical characteristics of the wolves, such as hunting and guarding, as well as life in family associations, are still present in every one of our house dogs. However, they are so accustomed to the help of the people that they have remained childlike wolves or wolves who live in deep symbiosis with humans.

A typical example: A wolf has taken a large piece of meat from a prey and is carrying it away to bury it. He is on the road for a while, starting to dig in a seemingly secure place, but then he changes his mind and continues to walk until he finds a really safe place. There he buries the prey with the snout. The domestic dog, who has just been given a big bone, wants to hide his prey even from supposed rivals. He passes through the garden, but finds no safe place in his opinion. Now he begins to howl to get his man to help him (which is amusing, the man approaches to help, the dog goes on immediately, since the man could possibly take away his prey, only to start again with the whining shortly afterwards).

He sees man as a sovereign leader in his family association, whom he can trust in difficult tasks. If a person fails in certain tasks, the dog feels himself to take over this task. A classic example is the expulsion of uninvited visit to the borders of the territory in the form of the postman. This stranger tries to penetrate the area constantly and is also greeted with joy by his man. Apparently, man does not recognize the prevalent danger. As humans communicate by voice, the dog begins to bark and has thus also success. After a short time, the intruder withdraws. If someone gets angry with the barking dog and shouts, the dog would understand this as a consensus in the expulsion bark.

In contrast to humans, most animals live very easy. They do not worry about mistakes in the past. Fear of the future is unknown to them. However, fears can be subconsciously influenced by experiences in the past and lead to an avoidance behavior, although there is no real danger. Dogs - or more generally developed animals - are still far ahead of humans in terms of mindfulness.

The dog is also an infantile wolf living in a human family whose characteristics are more or less pronounced depending on the breed. Even if he looks like a soft toy, this knowledge is essential for a mindful handling of one's own dog.

From his human being, he expects to be responsible for the provision of food, secure his own territory, and regularly roam the territory with him. He wants to participate in all these actions, but is grateful if the man takes over them. If the man shows weakness in his task-perception, the dog feels called to take over this part. He expects emotional stability from his human being. He does not understand moodiness.

What about dominance?

In many dog books it is taught that the dog has to subordinate himself to his human being. Therefore some "rules" have been developed. So the dog should never be elevated, not go before his person through doors, shall only get his food after man has eaten etc.

Failure to comply with these rules prompts the dog to take the lead role.

And there are even worse activities like the neck grip (which corresponds to the killing of a wolf) or the on-the-back roll (the funnily so-called "alpha roll"). Both of these measures can scare the dog to death and make him lose all his trust.

These rules were set up many decades ago. They result from artificially composed groups, some even of other animal species. In these compulsions, a "hacking order" (as observed in captured chickens) is formed, a hierarchy based on dominance exists. A wolf family, on the other hand, is not a compulsory community. The wolfs trust their parents, who care for them, occasionally get a little correction by the parents, but do not exert any reverent obedience to their parents (wolves don't know penalties).

The human-dog relationship is similar. Man is the sovereign leader to whom the dog can trust. While in puberty dogs also test limits, but no rituals are required in order not to lose the leadership claim.

Domination therefore has nothing to do with possible alpha leader properties, but rather is a question of individual dealings in concrete situations.

Dominance is a popular principle among people (and chimps and baboons). It is not only found in forced communities (as in prisons, barracks or ships), but is also found in hierarchical leadership systems and dictatorial forms of government. Man needs a king's crown, the dog does not.

Sovereignty is not produced by rituals of power, coercion or fear. A sovereign leader is like a solid rock in the surf, who in every situation preserves peace and can be trusted. Such a guide is desired by dogs (and, moreover, by humans).

A dominant leader is the opposite - the fear of loss of power is hidden by dominance. Watch the next time yourself, if you think you have to be dominant in front of your dog. Perhaps you recognize your own feelings of impotence.

Do dogs have conscience?

This question is again related to the subject of "dominance". I know a lot of dog owners who assure me that their dog had clearly bad conscience when they came home. In the search for the reason, he misses a cake in the kitchen, which the dog has eaten in the time of the absence of the man. Of course such an evil dog has to be punished (no, he does not have to !!).

But dogs still have no conscience in the sense of our morality. For the dog, the cake situation presents itself as follows: if the man is present, one can not eat the achievable cake. This immediately leads to anger. If the person is absent, the cake is reachable without anger. This corresponds to wolfish behavior. The piece of flesh belongs to that one, who can reach and devour it.

This is exactly what the dog does. The dog also knows from experience that an empty cake plate means trouble when the person comes back. Not because the dog was not allowed to eat the cake, but only because the sheet is empty. Now man comes home, the dog feels torn between rejoicing and fear, which he expresses by pronounced tail wagging. He would like to greet his people, but due to the impending anger, the dog shows calming signals (dodging etc.) that are interpreted by man as a clear sign of "bad conscience".

Bad conscience should in this case only have the man who has admitted this malaise.

How are dogs trained?

How are people educated? Through drill and punishment? This gives you cannon fodder for the front! Which teachers have you liked most? The authoritarian cholerics? Or was it more fun to learn when you were motivated? Which boss is more likely a leader? The patriarch or the charismatic?
Whom of these people would you trust more?

Learning is therefore fun when you are motivated by praise and you can trust the teacher. This principle is called positive reinforcement.

Dogs have great pleasure in learning. This is encouraged when the dog is praised for well-done behavior. The praise must immediately follow the action to be praised, otherwise the dog can no longer link it with its action. Therefore, the "clicker" has been introduced in dog education. Directly after a well-done action a clicking sound is triggered. This is followed by a reward. The dog gets to hear the click sound right after the correct execution, knows exactly that this action was correct and linked this signal positively with a reward. Of course you do not necessarily have to work with a "clicker", but the reward must be done 1-2 seconds after the correct action.

And if the dog does something wrong? Do not punish him. Always try to get the right action and then reinforce it positively with a reward. If the dog has proven itself in the practice, he does not have to be constantly rewarded; occasionally a rewards course can be omitted. This intermittent reward, as long as it does not produce too much frustration, is very conducive to later stages.

Penalties work very well in training. With fear, you can even get people to face the warfront and to be shot. Or you just keep the mouth in a totalitarian system and look away. But you will not be a convinced follower. You do not have much confidence in this master.

If the dog is punished, you will lose his confidence and possibly harm the relationship forever. A high price only for the dogs "nice" behavior. Perhaps the problem is more on the side of the punisher than the punished?

Whoever needs to work with punishments is weak and anything but a sovereign leader.

As I said, penalties work well, so still many dog schools work with it and give a success guarantee, which they can usually also keep. But the superficial functioning is costly because of anxiety and stress. Possibly the dog will bite in an extreme situation without warning.

A dog is also not a robot, which can be programmed at will. Whoever lives with a dog has embraced and accepted a living being with all its peculiarities, instead of shaping it according to his own ideas. This would not be done with a human partner. Humans would at least have the chance to escape, dogs are at their mercy.

Of course, there are very serious cases that can make living together impossible. Here you should visit a very experienced dog trainer, who has worked with the training method of positive reinforcement for many years. And of course, also has experience with the concrete problem. Or otherwise the far-sighted has to refer to a better colleague.

Unfortunately, so-called "educational aids" exist. There are, for example, "anti-bark" neckbands, which emit a water jet in the face by a sensor, if the dog barks. There might be other noises triggering this mechanism, and the dog is arbitrarily tormented. Perhaps a screaming child has triggered the mechanism and the dog now connects screaming children with a physical evil. The consequences are completely meaningless and dangerous.

Very popular are so-called "Haltis". These are collars similar to a horse's bridle. They are used when a dog pulls on a leash. Yes, of course it works, but there are smoother methods I would like to talk about later. I knew a dog, who had a completely oblique face. I thought he might have suffered a stroke that had so disfigured him. The keeper then told me that for many years he had used a Halti that had led to this sad face. The success remained despite Halti. The dog was hardly able to move with a leash. Very much patience was required to lead the dog again with a leash.

Also, choke collars, rattling tin cans etc. belong to this tyrannical accessory.

Have patience and compassion in raising your dog. Everything else has nothing more to do with mindfulness.

And accept the essence of a dog. Education does not mean the formation of a living being according to one's own ideas.

Why do dogs bark?

Wolves do not. They only howl to show their position to other wolves. Even dogs can howl. Sometimes this happens with sirens or music. If you are able to create the characteristic wolf's howl authentically and your dog agrees, you will experience a moment of highest connectedness.

Dogs have learned to communicate with humans through sounds. These sounds can vary in their loudness, frequency and tone sequence and thus attain quite different meanings. Once a "Wooff" can mean the request to open the door, a long-drawn "bow-wow" descending in pitch, begging for food or a salvage-like "wanwanwan" the alarm signal because of the invasion of a stranger.

Constant barking can be a sign of stress. A dog who is left alone relieves stress by barking and hopes to recall his man.

Rarely do dogs communicate with each other by barking. This usually only happens during a dog fight and dogs like humans shout each other.

What are calming signals?

Dogs communicate like wolves among themselves through body language. Although they try to do this with people, unfortunately, most people don't understand because of lack of mindfulness.

Wolves and dogs try to avoid conflicts. This has very economic reasons, because an injured body can no longer be used for hunting.

Dogs therefore use a very detailed system of body language to communicate their peacefulness to other creatures.

This is first of all looking away. When meeting other dogs, they don't move straight on, but get nearer to each other in curves.

Licking/tongue flicks, sniffing the ground, play bow, walking slowly, freezing, sitting down, yawning, wagging the tail and lying down can be other calming signals.

These signals are always to be seen in the context of a particular situation. Of course, dogs simply yawn because they are tired. Yawning can also be a displacement activity, that is an embarrassment gesture.

Unfortunately, bending over a dog or the straight look in the eye is a sign of aggression and leads to misunderstandings.

Nevertheless, dogs look very closely at their humans. Dogs are masters in observing and can already infer the emotions and intentions of humans by the smallest movements.

How do I know if a dog is aggressive?

Before a dog becomes aggressive, he first used calming signals unsuccessfully. Nevertheless, it happens that a dog bites without warning. Either he has a serious illness or he has had to learn over a long period that calming signals have no effect. A dog who is constantly annoyed, makes himself small, gets out of the way, yawns, licks himself over the muzzle and perhaps just because of this "strange" behavior is still further annoyed. Then he first shows his teeth and growls. This signal is also often neglected. At the very latest, people should be clear that they are responsible for an extreme malaise of the dog. The dog implored him to stop, or he would have to fight back. Often the human being sees the snarling of his person as a naughtiness and a lack of obedience of his dog and intensifies his negative actions. Probably the dog will now just snap. If this is also ignored, he will finally bite. Either the dog then bites out of fear (the ears are attached and the tail is drawn in), or he goes, which is very rare, with full aggression (here the ears are up and the tail is straight).

Many dogs are taken away the possibility of body language by mutilating their bodies (affectionately called "cropping") or by breeding their face so distorted that communication is no longer possible or even misunderstandings arise.

Should I get a dog?

After all the theoretical questions about the behavior of dogs, it is getting now more practical.

The choice of getting a dog is a very long-term decision. Some breeds can get 20 years old. During this period, costs for food, vaccinations, other medicines, routine examinations, surgeries, worm cures, claws and fur care, insurance and taxes will be incurred.

A dog, which by his very nature lives in a family, should never be left alone for more than four hours. Every day at least two walkings of several hours are required - with some breeds even more.

In the event of illness, the dog needs special care and may not be left alone. Traveling with a dog can become a problem as dogs are not allowed to be taken to many hotels, museums, restaurants.

What happens in one's own illness? Can the dog be taken care of?

In his old age the dog needs special care. It is possible that he is no longer clean. He can not spend the last and most difficult hour alone.

The rearing of a dog is considerably more complex than that of a child, which becomes independent at some time. Nevertheless, a dog is never a substitute for a child or a partner, because that would not correspond to his nature and he would suffer greatly under this blindness of his owner.

But with a dog one has a friend whom one seeks among the people in vain. No animal is closer to human than the dog.

Instead of long eulogies, I would like to briefly tell the story of Hachiko. Hachiko was an Akita and was born on November, 10th, 1923 in Odate, Japan. 1924 he was given to Professor Ueno who lived in Shibuya, Tokyo. The professor went to his university every day from Shibuya Station. In Shibuya, Hachiko waited each day for the return of his master. On May, 21st, 1925, Professor Ueno died in the university. Nevertheless, Hachiko continued to wait for his master's return until he died on March, 8th, 1935. In the meantime, the people at the train station cared for him, but they could not keep him from waiting for his professor. As early as 1934, a bronze statue was erected at Shibuya station. He is still very much honored in Japan today and is regarded as a symbol of loyalty.

Hachiko statue in Shibuya, Tokyo

Does the breed matter?

Dogs were first bred for different purposes. Hunting dogs are suitable for the tracking and chasing of game due to the incredibly good olfactory and hearing performance as well as endurance. Of course, a hunting dog, which is not allowed to carry out his original activity, must be specially employed.

Many breeds of hunting dogs are therefore handed over to hunters by their breeders.

Watchdogs see their task as particularly to protect their territory. Sheepdogs feel good only if they are able to cope with this task.

Particularly in the case of mixed breeds, one must pay attention to which breeds have mixed into the genetic material. According to Mendel's rules, these are not always directly recognizable in the immediately succeeding generation.

So the breed should always be adapted to your own interests and abilities. The size unfortunately says little about the characteristics of a dog. A small terrier used for hunting in fox caves, is very brave and has a lot of energy. His dear appearance does not at first suggest these qualities.

If you want to grow a breed dog, you should do this with a serious breeder who has time and space to look after the rearing of the dogs. He can also assess whether the chosen breed fits at all. Dog breeders, who breed large numbers of dogs exclusively for profit reasons should be strictly avoided because they are responsible for much suffering.

One should also refrain from encouraging the cultivation of agony breeding. Some breeds are extremely limited in their viability for optical reasons. An example: the Pug. Because of his facial shape, this poor creature is very short-winded. The eyeballs can be released from the eye socket by a strong pull (for example by a collar).

Dogs from animal protection are a good alternative if you want a slightly older dog. Animal shelters and organizations provide dogs. Often these dogs have been in the care of nursing homes or dog shelters. Therefore it is very often possible to get information about specific characteristics of the selected dog.

Even those who can not hold a dog themselves have the opportunity to offer dogs from shelters with a walk some variety in their dreary life.

When can I get a puppy home?

A puppy should not be separated from his mother and siblings under the age of 10-12 weeks. You should always get a blanket from the breeder, which still smells of his old family. The puppy should be able to get used to his new home.

At this age, puppies are in the midst of their socialization phase (ending slowly in the 16th week onwards). Here, the trust building to his/her human being is particularly important. But experiences with other animals and environments should also be made, as long as this has not already been done with the breeder. However, these experiences should not be made in a crash course but gentle and careful.

With a puppy you can already visit a puppy group, if this is moderated by experienced dog trainers. If a small dog is annoyed by other dogs, the damage is much greater than the supposed benefit. There is no general "puppy protection" under dogs.

Later, first courses or individual lessons can be booked, in which first commands, leash-walking, behavior on the street etc. can be practiced.

After the change of teeth (between the 4th and 7th month) puberty begins, which is often a very difficult time because the young dogs want to test their limits. This phase ends, depending on the breed of the dog, during the second year of life.

What supplies do I need for a dog?

- Leash (an extendible is indeed practical, but should be avoided first with pulling dogs)

- Harness (the dog should not be able to hatch out, therefore necessarily try different sizes)

- Name plate (at least with telephone number)

- Dog waste bags (so that the number of "dog-haters" does not get any bigger)

- Illuminating dog collar (Very useful for evening walks in free nature)

- Dog whistle

- GPS collar (in conjunction with SIM card and smartphone, a lost dog may be relocated)

- Dog water bottle (the cap forms a small bowl for on the road)

- Training Leash (for search games or education, later)

- Dog bag (for the transport of small dogs, for example in railway and airplane)

- Toys (best from natural rubber, so that nothing can be swallowed or teeth are damaged)

- Dog blanket (for on the go)

- Dog basket (should be placed in a place where the dog can rest without disturbance - but often he is looking for places where the basket does not fit, then helps the dog blanket again)

- Feeding bowls (one for constantly available water and one for food, both non-slip)

- Food, treats (later)

- First aid kit with tick tong (best to be carried along on walks)

- Brush, dog shampoo (long hairs require a special constant care, often only by a dog hairdresser)

- Dog car belt or box (the belt fulfills only the legal duty to prevent the dog from jumping around in the car - it does not provide protection for the dog in the case of accidents - only the car-mounted fixed dog box which is adapted to the size of the dog can help.)

- Liability insurance, health insurance with surgery and animal rescue (damage compensation and medical treatment can be very expensive, in some cases there are special animal rescue services, which can be joined as a sponsoring member.)

Which food is best for my dog?

In the case of dog food, you should take care that all additives are listed. Unspecified "animal components" can also be claws, etc. If the sum of all ingredients is not 100%, "fillers" may also be present in the dog's food. For very cheap varieties this could unfortunately also be grated car tires. On the other hand, some manufacturers achieve almost human food quality.

Dry food alone is very dull and should only be served with plenty of water. A good mixture of wet and dry food is certainly a good compromise.

Food remnants of human food should not be fed because they often contain spices that dogs can not tolerate. In particular, bones of chickens are dangerous as they can split.

A purely vegetarian food for dogs is also not recommended. Dogs are omnivorous, but sometimes require very high daily doses of certain minerals.

There are many opinions regarding the right food for dogs. If in doubt, consult a veterinarian.

What is toxic for dogs?

Many substances that humans tolerate can be harmful or lethal to dogs. Which includes:

Chocolate, alcohol, avocados, onions, garlic, coffee, tea, grapes, fruit cores, raisins, milk (products) and nuts.

Otherwise, human drugs are always toxic to dogs. And what is toxic to humans, is also for dogs.

If a dog has taken up dangerous substances, a veterinarian should be consulted immediately. This should also happen if he has eaten something unknown and shows signs of discomfort/ pain. A sample of the substance should be ensured. Forced vomiting should not be induced.

Unfortunately, it is often the case that dog-haters put down poisoned food (for example poisoned sausage). Therefore dogs should not eat anything unknown.

How do I give first aid to a dog?

Just like you would give it to humans. The dog is physiologically very similar to us as a mammal. In the case of an emergency, the responsivity must first be checked. If the dog is unresponsive, care must be taken to ensure that the trachea is free. Check breathing of the dog. If this is not the case, the dog must be given artificial respiration carefully over his nose. If pulse is no longer palpable (at the femoral artery at the hind leg near the hip), cardiopulmonary resuscitation must be given. The dog is alternately carefully respired, and chest compression on the dog lying on its right side (alternating 30 compressions and 2 breaths) must be given. The heart of the dog is at the place where the angled left elbow of the dog lies. This procedure may only be carried out in the absence of breathing and pulse and must not (never!) be practiced on a healthy dog.

Otherwise, the same rules apply to the first aid as on humans.

A special feature is the life-threatening twisted stomach (dog bloat) which can occur when a dog performs physical activity shortly after eating. Symptoms include restlessness, drooling, anxiety and the unsuccessful attempt to vomit. It is an extreme emergency which has to be treated immediately by a veterinarian.

A further anatomical peculiarity is in breeds with long spine (e.g. Dachshund, Basset). Movements such as jumping can lead to an injury and thus to permanent paralysis.

Disease is not always easy to detect in a dog. A dog who feels pain might withdraw, doesn't longer want to eat, and possibly licks the painful area. But he could also move around and yell. Also, a dog could bite immediately under pain. Here, special mindfulness is necessary in order not to interpret such behavior as a failure.

In all medical questions, a veterinarian should always be consulted, his telephone number always ready. Also, one should always think about the availability of animal clinics and animal emergency facilities.

How to house train a puppy?

If the first signs of restlessness are observed, the young dog should immediately be taken outside. If necessary, it must be carried out. If he did not make it on time, he should not be punished. The little mishap is removed without much attention.

If the dog has defecated outside, he must be praised for it. Remains of feces in the public are removed with the help of dog waste bags and fed to the waste.

Just at the beginning, this procedure must be repeated every few hours and requires patience. If after weeks no improvement has occurred, please consult a veterinarian.

Can I leave my dog home alone?

Dogs as social animals don't like to be alone. They would like to share all their activities with their family. Unfortunately this is not always the case. Many employers forbid dogs; in theaters, grocery stores and some restaurants, dogs are also not allowed. Although there is the possibility of leashing the dog in front of a shop on specially designed hooks, I strongly advise against it. The dog gets under stress in this situation, may start to bark and gets so in the visor of people who could annoy or even steal him in the worst case. To keep the dog in the car is also not a good advice, as the interior of the cars can heat up very quickly and this not only in the summer. Already many dogs have died.

So you should set up your house dog safe. All things that mustn't be chewed, or where the dog may be injured, should be removed. There should be his usual toys and a blanket that smells of his owner. Also water should always be provided.

First of all you should leave the house at short intervals and do not make any special farewells and greetings. If the dog is very restless when you leave, you may throw treats into the room before closing the door. So the dog is distracted first. Or he gets a chewing bone with which he is occupied for a long time.

If this should work, the intervals can be extended. However, do not leave your dog alone for more than 4 hours.

If all this does not work, there are dog daycares where your dog can stay and gets care for a paid time. It is necessary to pay attention to the length of the walks, the weather-proof accommodation and, in particular, the care of the dog group by dog trainers. A good dog daycare takes the time to show you its facilities.

How do you recognize a good dog school?

The trainer should not work with punishment. Even if he swears that his methods are tested and effective by domination theories - please avoid such people.

He should work according to the methods of positive reinforcement. The dog is praised for correct behavior, wrong behavior is ignored. Working with punishment is out of the question. Your mindfulness and compassion will ensure that you choose the right trainers and school. Think yourself about whether you want to learn something in such a school.

Good dog schools have a sufficiently large and well secured area. Several courses with small numbers of participants are offered for different knowledge levels. The dog trainers take enough time for each individual pupil and work especially lovingly with the dogs.

In the first course basic exercises are trained, questions about special cases are answered, later various games like agility, tracking search, mantrailing etc. are introduced.

For difficult cases the dog trainer offers individual lessons. Especially in such cases, the dog trainer should have long experience with such cases.

A good dog school teaches people about the nature of the dog and shows limits. They will never promise to shape the dog according to your ideas.

What should I do when the dog is pulling on the leash?

Do not worry, this is the standard problem when it comes to dog and leash and has been solved by generations of owners with their dogs.

First of all, you should ask yourself if it is really a problem. Perhaps the dog only pulls in the initial phase of the walk for happiness? Or he only pulls in certain situations, for example to reach other dogs or a certain area. One should clearly identify the situation before thinking about correcting this behavior.

The dog thus moves in any direction. Now, you should not pull on the leash yourself, since this could cause impulse injuries at the cervical spine. Rather, you should stop at first and then slowly change the direction and pull the dog carefully. So he has to learn that he can't decide about the right direction with his ideas of the right pace. If the dog pulls back, you must stop again. If the dog goes without pulling, he is immediately praised for it and gets a treat. With little patience the problem should be solved, whereby the training period can last a few weeks and setbacks can be experienced again and again.

An expandable leash would be a possible compromise. Possibly, however, the dog could just learn to pull by such a leash, since he pulls against the resistance of the reeling mechanism of the leash. The leash is therefore always under tension.

I am not a friend of consistently "walking at heel". Walking is for the dog the most exciting experience of the day, and you should give him plenty of time to sniff at different places and do his marks. If he has found an interesting track, you will be able to walk with him for a while - you will feel the pleasure of this common experience. Basically, you should always remain in mindful contact with your dog while on the walk and not be distracted by phone calls or similar. Also, you can give the decision to the dog, where he wants to go. He though will not dominate you forever.

Nevertheless, going "at heel" in rare cases may be useful in the short term (for example, in order not to have to leash the dog for a few seconds during an encounter). To practice this, you hold several treats in one hand and praise the dog with it when he goes directly to your side and keeps eye contact. For this purpose, the command "heel" is spoken.

What should I do when there is trouble with other dogs?

This is also a standard problem. Especially in our densely populated cities, there are always encounters of dogs with dogs. Often it can be seen in advance, whether the dogs like each other or anger is imminent. Perform the calming signal of evasion together with your dog, and make a large bow around the other dog. Ask the other, often undiscerning, dog owners to do so, too. At the encounter, shield your dog and praise him with treats if he ignores the other dog.

Very annoying are those people, who let your leashed dog meet with their free running dog. Ask that guy to leash on his dog and pass him in a bow. Normally, however, such an encounter also happens without major damage. If there is nevertheless a scuffle, the loosening of the leash can be the last salvation.

These situations imply considerable stress to the dog and can even lead to a loss of confidence. You can imagine this - we change the roles: your dog takes you on a leash through the city. Somewhere there are quite a lot of people. The dog therefore shortens the leash slightly, but the other people are close to you. Due to the short leash you can not avoid them. Eventually it happens - an extremely unpleasant guy comes close to you, wants to touch you, but the leading dog does not care. You shout to the unpleasant guy to get away, but he does not think about it. You get also shouted by your leading dog, after all, you should not behave so rude. This happens a few times until it is enough for you. The next unpleasant encounter goes then like this: knowing that you are not supported by your leading dog and have no way to escape, you simply attack the next obtrusive passant. The horror of your leading dog is great.

This is exactly what happens with your dog. At some point, your dog will give up if you do not support him in such encounters and will initiate a giant bark as soon as other dogs are encountered. If the dogs are too close, there may also be a scuffle.

You have trained the dog an unpleasant leash aggression, which now has to be dismantled with the above measures. Hopefully confidence in you will not be too much disturbed.

Should I have my dog castrated?

This is a very serious and emotional question that you must ultimately determine with your dog, yourself and your veterinarian.

If you want your dog for breeding, the question has become redundant.

Otherwise castration of the female and male dog can be considered (castration is the total removal of the internal reproductive organs).

The surgery leads to a change in the personality of the dogs. They may be a bit quieter. Male dogs lose sexual stress. It is also not so stressful for him to constantly check the marking of his territory.

Female dogs are no longer chased by male dogs because of the lack of heat, and there is no risk of false pregnancy. The risk of some diseases may be reduced.

Alternatively, a hormone treatment would also be conceivable.

These are just small thoughts. Please discuss this topic with your veterinarian.

What games are right for dogs?

Even adult dogs are very fond of playing. Many dogs enjoy dog sports (agility) where obstacles have to be overcome.

For almost all dogs are search games the greatest. Dogs experience their world mainly through the nose. It is the greatest pleasure for them, to use the sense also for the purpose of finding a treat.

A very simple game is to hide various treats in a room while the dog is waiting outside the door. He will be very restless in anticipation, perhaps already in a typical game position (play bow). As soon as the door is opened, he rushes in and finds the first hidden treats by tracking. For some complicated hiding places, he will need longer time and - as an infantile wolf - he may look at you, pat and ask for help. Let him have some more time and give him the success to have solved the task independently.

The treats can also be hidden in small boxes. Now you can experience how it is when the little wolf kills its prey. He will pack the box with his mouth and shake it vigorously. This is nothing else but the neck bite for killing prey, which is then shaken to death (I know - unpleasant - but dogs are, like their ancestors, predators). Then he will shred his prey to reach the treats.

The king discipline of games is mantrailing. Here runs a person equipped with a special treat a path over a longer distance and goes out of the sight of the dog. The dog now gets a spur probe of the target person under the nose and receives the command "search". Already at the first time he will intuitively know what to do. It is important that the dog is connected to his mantrailing guide by a harness and a training leash. If the dog has found the target person, he is particularly praised and immediately receives his treat.

This search game is very stressful and should therefore be interrupted by short breaks between the individual trails. In addition, the dog should always drink sufficient water.

The trails can become more complex after time. If only short and straight trails were tracked on the forest floor, the trails become longer and more complicated. Later on, you can do it on a a more difficult surface like asphalt. It is particularly difficult when rain and wind blow away the small particles of the body that scatter the target person on his way.

Hounds like Beagles and Bloodhounds are especially suited for this game. But you can do it with every dog. You will experience your dog in the greatest joy, and he will then fall asleep satisfied and exhausted.

Are throwing and pulling games suitable?

Obviously these games are also very funny for dogs. However, you have to know that the dog initially builds up positive stress, which after a certain time turns into negative stress. The organism is overstrained. For the observer, however, it looks like as the dog still has a lot of fun.

Therefore, you should not use this kind of games too often and only for a short time.

A similar type of stress reduction is chasing his own tail. This also leads to negative stress. If you observe these stereotypes, it is necessary to analyze where the original stress for the dog initiates.

There is the opinion that pulling games would promote the dominance of a dog if you let him win all the time. As described above, the dog will not start a revolution because of winning, and will not feel like a leader over his people. It makes sense, however, to use the "off" command (see below) during dripping, so that, for example, objects can be taken away which he is not supposed to have.

How do I teach "sit" and "down"?

These are the basic exercises taught in every dog school. It is important to get the dog to sit or lay down in special situations. They are very easy to teach.

Sit: The dog is standing. A treat is held in one hand in front of the dog's nose and it is lifted slowly. To reach it, he will automatically move into the completely natural sitting position. At this moment you say the command "sit" and give the dog the treat.

Down: This works almost exactly, except that the hand now goes deeper. First, the dog will get up again and bend down to the hand. He must then return to the sitting position and follow the hand until he comes into the laying position. Then say the command "down" and the dog gets his treat. Also this position is a natural dog position.

Please take care not to get the dog to "sit" and "down" in cold and wet places.

Like every exercise, this is learned quickly in non-irritating environments. If the dog is later in the company of other dogs and there is much exciting to see, he seems to have forgotten everything. Here has the exercise to be repeated with great patience.

The dog should maintain a position until it is ended with another command, like "go". Of course, he is also praised for it.

Even with these spoken commands, gestures can be used, since dogs understand body language much better than words.

What commands are also important?

Of course, it is one of the most important commands to call the dog back to yourself. For this purpose, "come" can be used. Curl the dog with a treat. Once he has arrived, he is praised and given the treat. If the dog does not come immediately, it makes no sense to shout at the dog impatiently. Be careful. The screaming is just expressing your anger and scares the dog. Also the mantra-like repetition of "come" is not really useful, when the dog though does not come. Again, prefer to work with gestures.

A variation is the command "stay". The dog is called into the sitting position, then move away and show the dog by body language that he should not move (usually a defending hand). Say the command "stay". The exercise is cancelled as soon as the dog runs away on his own. He is neither scolded nor punished for it, but gets simply no treat and has to repeat the exercise. This is the way of positive amplification.

As already mentioned, the observation of commands becomes particularly difficult, if there is something much more interesting. But sometimes the dog must immediately return to his person. He could, for example, run in the direction of a busy street. Many dogs get killed by passing a road. For this purpose, the super-come-command must be trained. Usually, however, this will be used when the human being is already emotionally mixed-up. Here would a loudly roared "come" be more contraproductive. Therefore, it is better to use a whistle. The dog must learn that the whistle instantly means the delivery of an absolute super-treat, which he would never get otherwise. This command must be practiced regularly to make it work.

The dog whistle could also be used as an "off" command. If the dog finds something that he is not supposed to eat, this could be the command for him, to give the "catch" back and thus being replaced by the super-treat. The problem is that the dog actually sees the catch as his "prey" and is therefore not ready for an (also economically sensible) exchange. Therefore the "off" command, whether spoken or with dog whistle, requires a lot of practice.

The "no" command is a very bad word. Instead of a negative command, use a positive substitute like "sit". Pay attention to how much the dog is showing calming signals on "no" or, generally, angrily pronounced commands.

What do I do when the dog goes out for hunting?

It can not be said often enough. The domesticated wolf, our dog, likes to chase as well as his ancestor. In particular, hunting is a self-rewarding behavior. Just tracking a trail gives the dog's brain an euphoric uplift. The chase is much more attractive than the catch. If your dog chases a rabbit, and you would lure him with a finely prepared roast rabbit, which could immediately comfortably be eaten, this would hardly work.

How also to deal with hunting? You do not always want the dog leashed. You should do this anyway, especially if game (and the inevitable hunter) are nearby. Hunters like to shoot unleashed dogs because they think they are poaching.

If the dog runs free, he should always be near to his human. He should not leave the sphere of activity of his human. For achieving this, however, human activity must be attractive. How would it be, for example, if only his human suddenly discovers a tree where many sausages grow? The dog will be enthusiastic and likes to stay by your side as he hopes that you will make many other similar discoveries.

In addition, he should be regularly praised not to leave the humans sphere of activity.

If this does not work, because the dog does not want to come or runs at other directions and does not respond to "come" With treats, you could try an exercise with a training leash. The dog is hung on a long (10 meters) training leash, so that he can not escape. If the dog is inattentive, hide yourself. If the dog comes back and finds you, then he is of course praised.

And when it tough had happened that the dog is away on a chase? It is the best to wait for the dog at the place of separation. Always call his name repeatedly (or better track his position using GPS). If the dog then returns after a long period of waiting, he is - of course - praised. If he is now being shouted or punished, he will consider very carefully the next time whether it is worth returning to his human.

What do I do when visitors are welcomed too enthusiastic?

I waited to answer this question until the end, since I get always in trouble with this situation. The dog wants to welcome a favored person by licking the face. This is a highest sympathy gesture I enjoy very much. Unfortunately, this is not for everyone. And the dog owner argues that he does not want to allow exceptions. Finally, Grandma Schmeltzer had almost fallen to the ground on the last enthusiastic greeting.

What also to do? If the dog wants to jump up, he can be welcomed in a friendly way, but turn away and alternatively give your hand for a welcome. If this process is still too enthusiastic, you can try to lure the dog into the sitting position, praise him, and then let him perform his hand-grasping ritual.

A similar situation is loud barking when the door bell goes. Here also the dog can be lured into the sitting position, then rewarded with treats. Or you can turn it off with a delicious rain of treats.

Barking is a natural reaction of the dog as someone approaches his territory. Distraction maneuvers with reward are an appropriate response to this behavior. Here, the "naughty" barking is not praised, even if the human being likes to interpret it so.

It is often claimed that the visitor should never be greeted first by the dog because it promotes dominant behavior. As mentioned several times before, there is no need to worry about the leadership role. Of course you can let the dog sit first and only do the greeting after giving a command. However, the dog will not understand this behavior and will be frustrated. Here also makes the mindful middle way sense.

Epilogue

By this small booklet I wanted to give you a brief insight into the nature of dogs and make you more mindful about the most common questions and mistakes.

Mindful handling means to accept the dog as a dog and not to shape it according to your own ideas. This is appropriate animal husbandry.

Go on. Buy the recommended books, look for a dog school, where your dog is not punished and watch mindfully.

Should you have fallen in love with the Zen way, perhaps this Koan may help you: "To Master Joshu came a monk and asked him if a dog has Buddha-nature or not. Joshu answers: Mu." (Meaning of "Mu": nothing/the question arises from a dualistic mind/emptiness).

Thanks

Without the contact to these people, this little book had never been written:

Rita Kampmann, dog school "Freude am Hund", Munich, Germany, and her team (especially Diana) Thanks for the dog trainer apprenticeship.

Thomas Riepe, teacher of dog psychology, Anröchte, Germany Thanks for the knowledge about wolves.

Annette Gräff, "Dog Daycare at the Olympiapark Munich", Germany, and her team (especially Sorina) Thanks for the many beautiful hours in the dog garden and the possibility of observation.

Clarissa von Reinhardt, "animal-learn", Bernau am Chiemsee, Germany

Thank you for the books from animal-learn. All books can be recommended without restriction.

Thich Nhat Hanh, Zen Master

Thank you for books, Dharma lectures and retreats.

... and thanks to all the many dogs - I've learned so much from you

Mali, Clara, Yoda, Tyson, Sina, Arthur, Bosse, Eddie, Ludwig, Pia, Hector, Buddy, Nelson, Nuscha, Hudson, Barney, Paula, Nicki, Lea, Branko, Alois, and many others.

Recommended reading

Dogs:

Eaton, Dominance in Dogs

Rugaas, Calming Signals

Rugaas, DVD: Calming Signals

Zen and Buddhism:

Hendriksson, The Secret Book of Zen

Junghardt, Satori

Thich Nhat Hanh, The Heart of Buddhas Teaching

Tolle, A New Earth

Tolle, The Power of Now

Mali

1990 - 2008